Welcome to Winchester Cathedral

THIS IS A LIVING CATHEDRAL. Its story is more the biography of a continuing life than a catalogue of far-off events. It is a biography that includes times of glory and times of desolation; the developments, the enrichments, the scars and the improvements, all here for us to read.

The living pulse of it was already there at the time that it was first built. The Norman castle, on the hill above, dominated the city; the Bishop's castle was on Wulf's Island (Wolvesey), and on the floor of the valley between them lay the monastery and its cathedral, with the huddle of houses lining the warrens of the city surrounding it. For it was said then that it was the role of the knights to fight and to rule, of the peasants to work and of the monks to pray.

It is that steady pulse of prayer for the ever-changing society and world in which it is set that is still the heartbeat of this living church.

DEAN OF WINCHESTER

ABOVE: A verger holds a processional cross, formed in the shape of the risen Christ, made by a contemporary sculptor and given in memory of a much-loved member of the congregation in 2000.

RIGHT: The great central porch of the cathedral forms part of the first phase of the 14th-century re-modelling of the west front by Bishop William of Edington. These doors, and their predecessors, have opened for distinguished visitors and liturgical processions for over 900 years.

The Cathedral and its Buildings

VISITORS, PILGRIMS AND V.I.P.s alike usually approach the cathedral from the heart of the city, along the tree-lined paths that cross the green lawns of the Outer Close to come out into the open space before the west front of this, the longest medieval cathedral in Europe. The view being dominated by the present cathedral, it is easy to overlook the ground plan, here marked out in brick, of the Old Minster, the earlier Saxon cathedral (begun about AD 648) which was replaced by the Norman cathedral and finally demolished in 1093 when the new building and old converged.

The old Saxon church was demolished by Bishop William Walkelin, and much of the stonework of the Old Minster incorporated in the new building. The remains of St Swithun, royal burials and the relics of Saxon saints from Old Minster were later given an honoured place in the new cathedral.

An inscribed stone on a wall flanking the space before the west front records that the original Norman west front, framed by two towers, once extended much further. Any later intention to rebuild the former western structure in a more contemporary style would have been frustrated by the Black Death in 1348, which halved the population of Winchester, reduced the number of monks from 60 to 32 and drastically reduced the monastery's income from its estates. It was through the generosity of Bishops Edington 1346–66 and Wykeham 1367–1404 that the three west porches and the great west window were created as a new west end to close off the truncated cathedral.

ABOVE: Following an extensive research excavation carried out during the 1960s and '70s, the footprint of the Anglo-Saxon predecessor to the present cathedral was uncovered. The brick outline on the north side of the nave shows its extent and complexity.

LEFT: The approach to the west front of the cathedral from the city, through the avenue of lime trees.

OPPOSITE: The great west front of Winchester Cathedral has been greeting pilgrims and visitors for over 900 years. In its present form it dates from the 14th century.

THE INNER CLOSE

On the south side of the cathedral, reached through a narrow passageway to the south of the west front, lies the Inner Close, from earliest times the domestic area of monastery and cathedral life. Some traces of the Great Cloister and Lesser Cloister of monastic days remain, many incorporated, and so lost to view, in later buildings.

On the eastern side, five pillared arches form the entrance to what was once the Chapter House, now a green space, where the monks met to establish tasks for the day, deal with issues requiring decision or discipline and to hear the Prior reading and expounding some portion of the monastic rule of St Benedict, under which they lived.

Alongside the Chapter House, the raised Dean Garnier garden occupies the site of the dormitory from which the monks passed into the south transept for mattins at 2 o'clock in the morning. Their rule required them to sleep fully clothed to be ready for this night office, but sandals were set aside and also the knives they carried for eating and general purposes, "lest they roll on them in the night and suffer an injury". Abutting the dormitory on the south east side were the monks' wash place and lavatory, irrigated by a branch of the Lockburn, which now travels underground through a vaulted conduit into the main stream beyond the cathedral to the east.

BELOW: The Inner Close is enclosed on the south and east by the nave and the south transept. The lawn in the foreground would have been surrounded by the monastery's Great Cloister.

LEFT: The south transept (1079–93) towers over the cathedral library, the chapter house arcade and the Dean Garnier garden.

BELOW: The south elevation of the nave was remodelled into 12 perpendicular gothic bays from the original 14 Norman ones in the 14th and 15th centuries.

ABOVE: The Deanery Long Gallery, with its open loggia underneath, was built in 1673 by Dean Clarke, "at his own expense". The size of the Deanery after the Commonwealth must have been considered too modest for a post-Restoration Dean.

BELOW: Cheyney Court and the Porter's Lodge are timber-framed buildings surviving from the late 15th and early 16th centuries. Cheyney Court (the two gables on the left) accommodated the bishop's court in which he exercised his jurisdiction over the area of Winchester known as The Soke. The gate, with its splendid wisteria, is of the same date and retains its original oaken doors.

The Deanery, canonical houses and Dome Alley

The first prominent building on the east side of the Inner Close is the Prior's Hall, with its five tall gothic windows set between buttresses. Around the south end of the hall, and set back, are the three arches opening onto a fragment of 13th-century cloister, which incorporates Roman paving found elsewhere in the Close. This is the entrance to the Dean's (formerly the Prior's) lodging. Here distinguished visitors were accommodated – Henry VII's oldest son, Prince Arthur, was born here and Philip of Spain stayed here before his marriage to Mary Tudor; visitors and residents, retainers and pensioners sat together in the Prior's Hall for the main meal of the day.

Set back, but visible above the garden wall to the right, is a long gallery with an open loggia beneath it, built by Dean Clarke, re-using an older window, which, no doubt, provided a wet-weather promenade for Charles II. The King was a frequent visitor at the time when he visited the races and was planning to build the English answer to Versailles at Winchester. The Peninsular Barracks up the hill to the west of the city incorporate the buildings that he began before his death.

Beyond the Deanery and further to the east is the Pilgrims' Hall – the title declares its purpose – now just three bays of the earliest hammer-beam roof are in existence. The school (The Pilgrims' School), in addition to its new buildings, incorporates a former canon's house and the half-timbered range of the priory stable block.

Bridging the space between the stable block and the gateway beyond is a half-timbered building with a fine wisteria. Known as Cheyney Court, this was, until 1851, the bishop's Manorial Court where tenants of his estates would come to claim their rights. The part closest to the gate was the porter's lodge.

St Benedict was very clear about the character and duty of a porter at this or any other of the principal entrances to his monasteries: not a young man who would always want to be somewhere else, but a steady fellow who, day or night, in season or out of season, would "welcome visitors as God's guests". That phrase is still remembered in the cathedral as setting the standard for service.

On the south side of the Close is a handsome house, the 'Judges' Lodgings' (the

ABOVE: Izaak Walton, best known as the author of *The Compleat Angler*, was Steward to George Morley, Bishop of Winchester (1662–84) and lived with his daughter and son-in-law at No. 7 The Close. When he died in 1683 he was buried in a chapel in the south transept, now known as The Chapel of St John and the Fishermen Apostles. The window in the chapel which shows Walton in contemplation by the River Itchen at Winchester was given in his memory in 1914.

flag is flying when a judge is in residence). Beyond it continues a street of 17th-century canons' houses on an axis that leads from the top of Dome Alley, past the end of the Pilgrims' Hall, along an apple walk to the Lockburn and across the Lockburn to the Bishop's Palace of Wolvesey. The area from the beginning of the apple walk is not open to the public. It was in one of these houses that the ageing Izaak Walton lived with his daughter and son-in-law.

The distinguished buildings on the west side of the Inner Close were also canons' houses before the number of canons and the extent of their domestic households were scaled down to the more modest establishments of today.

The view from the top of the cathedral tower offers a wonderful, overall survey of Inner and Outer Close and the whole city.

Standing outside the west front of the cathedral, what do people expect to find if they take the next step and come inside? A great church certainly: built, enlarged, refashioned and adorned by bishops with a vision for it and the work of many craftsmen, their names mostly no longer remembered but whose own skill and imagination contributed so much to this wonderful building. There will be memorials to the famous and also memorials to those whose names might too easily be forgotten. Here, too, is evidence of the faith and mission, the skill and contribution of many whose names are unknown to us. There is much to discover and to stir a sense of wonder. But in the end, the hope is that the cathedral does not simply engage curiosity but is known as a living cathedral where prayer has been valid, and still is.

LEFT: The south transept with the 'lean-to' addition that now houses the cathedral library, the 'slype' or tunnel underneath and the chapter house arcade. Wolvesey, the bishop's house, is in the distance.

OVERLEAF: Winchester Cathedral from the north-west showing the west front, the tower, the north transept and the immense length of the nave.

Inside the Cathedral

TO ENTER THE CATHEDRAL and to stand looking along the vault is to behold the spine of this great church. To look at eye level towards the nave altar and then beyond it, through the quire screen to the high altar, is to be gazing into the heart of it, to the bread and wine, which are consecrated and distributed at those altars, and to the prayers offered, received and answered day by day. Here is that heartbeat of this great church, the daily, regular pulse of prayer.

Among the many who have travelled this route are those whose stories catch the imagination. We can see William the Conqueror poring over the plans of the cathedral that his kinsman (William Walkelin) was building; and his son, William Rufus, who came here wearing his crown at Easter, and was some years later brought in a carrier's

RIGHT: The purbeck 'marble' and limestone tomb in the centre of the quire. Long thought to be that of William II (Rufus), killed in a hunting accident in the New Forest in 1100, modern scholarship has argued that it is the tomb of Henry of Blois, Bishop of Winchester 1129–71.

OPPOSITE: Looking east down the nave. The architecture was transformed in the 14th and 15th centuries at the expense of successive Bishops of Winchester from the original three-tiered Norman elevation (which is still visible in the transepts) to the soaring Perpendicular Gothic nave that we see today.

RIGHT: Mary Tudor, daughter of Henry VIII and Catherine of Aragon, was married to Phillip of Spain in the cathedral in July 1554. This X-frame armchair, now in the Triforium Gallery, is traditionally thought to have been the chair in which she sat during the ceremony.

BELOW: The Triforium Gallery is situated high in the south transept of the cathedral, above the cathedral library, and displays sculpture, woodwork and metalwork from 1100 years of the cathedral's history. The strength of the collection is the remarkable assemblage of late 15th-century sculpture that survives from the Great Screen.

BELOW: Jane Austen died in Winchester in July 1817 and is buried in the north nave aisle. Although her gravestone makes no mention of her prowess as an author, her writings are commemorated on a brass on the aisle wall and in a window above.

cart from the New Forest, where he had been killed, to be buried under the tower. Here, too, came Henry IV to be married to Joan of Navarre, and Mary Tudor and Philip of Spain for their marriage. Henry of Winchester, born here in 1207 and later known as Henry III, was more probably baptised in the Castle, but Prince Arthur, the first son of Henry VII (and of the new Tudor dynasty) was certainly brought here to be baptised, in that name laying claim to inherit the riches of British history. Through a neighbouring door and down that nave, the marauding parliamentarian troops rode or made their clamorous way to desecrate the quire and make off with treasures of fabric and manuscripts, using the bones of kings and prelates to break the windows. And it was here, following the return of Charles II to rule after the death of Oliver Cromwell, that a new bishop, dean and canons came to restore the cathedral to its function as a great church. Here, much later (July 1817), the body of Jane Austen was brought to burial in the north aisle quietly before morning prayer.

THE NAVE

These days, the great nave (from the Latin for ship, navis) is largely full of chairs and it is natural to assume that so vast a space was created to accommodate a large congregation. But the monks held their services in the quire and the nave was empty. Winchester people worshipped in their own churches, but they could stand with pilgrims in the nave to overhear the monks singing their offices in the quire, or to be present when any mass was said in Wykeham's chantry or at the altar before the screen, drawn there when the ringing of a bell advised them that bread and wine had again become the body and blood of Christ.

The chantry chapel for William of Wykeham, who transformed the Norman nave to its present form, is part way down the nave. That of William of Edington, who preceded him and began the work, is near the nave altar, originally in a reserved space between a rood screen and the entrance to the quire, at the place where the monks gathered before entering the quire to sing and say their offices.

Before Edington (d.1366) made a modest start on altering the west front, and William of Wykeham (d.1404) dramatically transformed the nave, the visitor would have seen the heavy pillars and rounded arches of the Norman nave rising

OPPOSITE: A view west from the tower showing the nave roof and the pinnacles of the west front.

BELOW: The effigy of William of Wykeham, Bishop of Winchester (1367–1404). It lies on his tomb-chest inside his chantry chapel on the south side of the nave. The effigy is of painted alabaster and shows him in his full bishop's robes, angels at his head and, at his feet, three Benedictine monks, perhaps those chosen to say masses for the repose of his soul.

BELOW: The nave vaulting at Winchester, in a style known as 'stellar lierne', is unique and dates principally from the 15th century. Here we see it in evening light with the west window, and the heraldic and decorative bosses at the intersection of the vault-ribs.

OPPOSITE: The vault-ribs spring from the decorative capitals terminating the wall-shafts that divide each bay of the nave.

on either side in three tiers to support the roof, which was made of timbers stripped from the Conqueror's hunting forest (donated in a rash moment), now known as the New Forest. The three tiers of the Norman structure can still be seen in the north transept.

Wykeham transformed the round Norman arches into tall, perpendicular ones, creating a vault and an upper range of windows above them. He also opened great windows in the side aisles, so that the building became flooded with coloured light. His arms, those of his diocese, the Royal Arms and St George's Cross can all be seen high on the vault together with roses, foliage and faces contributed by the genius of his craftsmen.

Wykeham's chantry, containing an effigy and an altar where masses were said for his soul, is mid-way down the nave on the south at a place where, during his Winchester childhood, he attended a mass said by a favourite monk called Richard Pekis. Almost opposite is the font that was in the cathedral before he was born.

ABOVE: The font is usually dated to around 1150–60 and attributed to the generous patronage of Henry of Blois, Bishop of Winchester (1129–71). It is made of black 'marble' (actually a dark limestone) from Tournai in Belgium and is carved with scenes from the life of St Nicholas, as well as other symbolic and decorative roundels.

The font

The font of black, Tournai 'marble' (late 12th-century), still used to baptise young and old alike, shows carved scenes from the life of St Nicholas. Facts about Nicholas (Bishop of Myra in what is now Turkey) are few. Legends were legion, so much so that his remains were 'liberated' from obscurity to be installed in the church in Bari, southern Italy, on 9 May 1087, before a well-chosen audience of church dignitaries, including the then exiled Archbishop of Canterbury, St Anselm. It was the ecclesiastical equivalent of winning the World Cup. The resultant worldwide devotion to St Nicholas gathered in pawnbrokers, sailors, Russians, Greeks and very many others. One story (shown here) is that he slipped money into a house to spare a nobleman the indignity of putting his daughters on the street.

THE TRANSEPTS AND THEIR CHAPELS

What was this cathedral like before a bishop who was born and baptised in Winchester transformed it? The north transept tells the story, for it is here that the massive, three-tier structure of the original Norman cathedral can still be seen clearly. Here, too, is evidence of further projects that were never completed, if only because the ground and its high water table provided inadequate foundations. The flanking towers to the north were never built. The central tower that bridged the quire collapsed and was rebuilt with massive, unshakeable piers: not the merest suggestion of a spire now rises above it. To some extent the size of these piers is disguised by the great wall of painted timber, currently covered by silk banners, that fills the great arch and supports the organ pipes.

BELOW: The ceiling in the north transept, designed in the Tudor style, was inserted in 1819. The Christus figure by the contemporary sculptor Peter Eugene Ball was given to the cathedral in 1990.

ABOVE: The organ case on the north side of the quire was designed in 1825 by Edward Blore and contains much of the Henry Willis organ exhibited at the Great Exhibition of 1851, although rebuilt and added to on many occasions.

RIGHT: Military memorials in the south nave aisle.

OPPOSITE: A view of the south transept ceiling, in the Tudor style, inserted in 1819. Hanging from the ceiling is one of a pair of splendid brass chandeliers given to the cathedral by Dean Cheyney in 1756. The other hangs in the high altar sanctuary.

The Holy Sepulchre Chapel

Beneath the organ case is the Holy Sepulchre Chapel, which retains, by chance, the finest 12th-century wall paintings in the country. The original vault was changed in the 13th century – the east wall covered over and its design replicated on a new layer of plaster. A fall of plaster in the 19th century disclosed a fragment of what lay beneath. But it was only with the development of reliable techniques in the 20th century that restorers uncovered the original painting on the east wall under the new layer, which has now been removed to the opposite end of the chapel.

Here, where the dead Christ is shown laid in the tomb, we lay the names of those we have known and loved on 'All Souls Day', asking that they may be raised with him into the eternal purposes of God.

RIGHT: The Epiphany Chapel, with windows designed by Edward Burne-Jones and made by the William Morris workshop, was created in the western aisle of the north transept between 1907 and 1910.

The Epiphany Chapel

Also in the north transept is the Epiphany Chapel with its windows made by (William) Morris & Co., some designed by Edward Burne Jones. Its modern glass, engraved by Tracey Sheppard, commemorates cathedral links with Holy Trinity Rangoon, Namirembe in Uganda, the Duomo in Florence, the monastery of Fleury, St Swithun's Stavanger and St Nicholas Newcastle, and recalls the gathering of our partners at the Millennium. Embroidered cushions represent the arms of the Channel Islands, which became part of the diocese in 1499, formerly belonging to the Diocese of Coutances in Normandy.

OPPOSITE: The Holy Sepulchre Chapel in the north transept is decorated with the finest 12th-century wall paintings in England. The east wall is painted with scenes of the deposition and entombment of Christ and dates from 1170–80. Later, in the 13th century, the figure of Christ and other scenes were painted on the newly-constructed vault.

LEFT: A limestone roundel of the *Agnus Dei* or Lamb of God by the English, 20th-century sculptor Eric Gill. It was installed in the Epiphany Chapel in the north transept in 1993.

RIGHT: The chapel of St John and the Fishermen Apostles, for many years a vestry and store room, was restored to liturgical use in 1996. The altar furniture was designed and made by the contemporary sculptor Peter Eugene Ball and the seating by Alison Crowther.

FAR RIGHT: The Lady Chapel, with the east window by C.E. Kempe, inserted to commemorate the Diamond Jubilee of Queen Victoria, the reredos in memory of the Hampshire writer Charlotte Yonge, and the Pietà by Peter Eugene Ball.

BELOW: The Guardian Angels chapel is in the north-east corner of the cathedral. This is a view of the vault, painted with angels between 1225 and 1230 and partially repainted between 1260 and 1280.

Side chapels

There are several more side chapels in addition to the Holy Sepulchre Chapel, the Epiphany Chapel and the chantry chapels. On the eastern side of the north transept there is evidence of three former chapels. At the eastern end of the cathedral, the central Lady Chapel is flanked by the Guardian Angels' Chapel on the north side and another, now dominated by the tomb of Thomas Langton, on the south side. In the south transept is the Venerable Chapel and the Fisherman's Chapel, with the grave of author Izaak Walton.

There are so many chapels because in the past, many of the monks were also priests who had an obligation to say mass daily at one altar or another, and accumulated further obligations to say masses for the dead. The different chapels are still used on weekdays, and the chantry chapels on the anniversary of those remembered there.

William Walker

Along with the mortuary chests, with their reminder of kings and bishops, and the memorials to many who did much for the construction and glorification of the cathedral, the largely anonymous builders, stonemasons and craftsmen have their own commemoration in the great fabric of the cathedral itself. But in recent times, one of them has been given his own memorial among the great by the Lady Chapel in the retroquire – William Walker. When the timber foundations were seriously undermined as the peat beneath was compressed, and the building began to break its back, he was the diver who went down through the water to underpin the foundations with concrete and to save it. His work (1906–11) is rightly remembered. But let his memorial also be a reminder of those anonymous workers to whom the cathedral owes its construction and conservation.

ABOVE: A 'poppy head' or desk-end from the late 15th-century stalls in the Lady Chapel, depicting two monkeys. Much of the decorative detail of the stalls was sympathetically restored in the 1890s.

RIGHT: The Pietà in the Lady Chapel, Mary with the dead Christ across her knees, is the work of the contemporary sculptor Peter Eugene Ball and was given to the cathedral by the Roman Catholic congregation in Winchester in 1990.

25

THE CRYPT AND THE PILGRIMS' STEPS

ABOVE: A contemporary sculpture, *Sound II* by Antony Gormley (1986), was installed in the Crypt in 1993. Conceived as a sculpture to stand in water, it is seen to best advantage when the crypt floods during the winter months.

In the north transept, the door down into the crypt takes the visitor into the mysterious depths of the building. The crypt is often flooded for much of the year, the water rising in a well placed immediately below the high altar and through the floor of the crypt itself. When it is flooded, the vault and its sculpture by Antony Gormley, *Sound II*, his gift to the Cathedral unveiled in 1993, form a wonderfully contemplative scene.

But we follow the pilgrims, for it was from the north transept that pilgrims made their way up the Pilgrims' Steps. They crossed the astonishing 'carpet' of patterned tiles to arrive in the spacious area of the retroquire, in essence itself a hall church created by Bishop Godfrey de Lucy (d.1204), and the shrine that they had come to find. Many of the tiles in this area are original and over 800 years old.

OPPOSITE: The original tile 'carpet' in the retroquire dates from the 13th century. These are clay tiles, inlaid with a coloured slip and glazed. There are many designs, some heraldic and some decorative. It is the largest indoor area of medieval tiles to survive in England.

BELOW: The crypt at Winchester Cathedral dates from the earliest building phase of 1079–93. It is Anglo-Norman architecture at its most spare.

THE QUIRE

The quire is enclosed on the north and south by the quire stalls and the masonry behind them, and towards the east by stone side screens created by Bishop Fox and glazed later, with his Latin motto and his arms depicting a pelican. These screens also separate the quire from the north and south presbytery aisles. Each screen is terminated by either a chantry – Bishop Fox (1501–28) on the south – or a chapel – Bishop Gardiner on the north – where the two aisles open into the space of the retroquire.

Monks coming from their separate activities about the monastery for prayer ('the Office') gathered by Bishop Edington's chantry chapel to enter the quire together as a community, already united in its focus on its Lord who would be both the origin and the aim of their worship.

OPPOSITE: This is the heart of the cathedral. A view from the high altar steps looking through the presbytery and quire, down the nave to the west window. On the left is the 19th-century bishop's throne or *cathedra*, the Latin word from which 'cathedral' derives.

RIGHT: The presbytery screens are dated by inscription to 1525, therefore inserted into the three bays either side of the presbytery during the episcopacy of Richard Fox. On top of the screens, three on each side, are six remarkable 'mortuary chests', which contain the bones of pre-conquest monarchs and bishops as well as, according to an inscription, the bones of William II (Rufus) whose burial in the cathedral in 1100 reputedly caused the crossing tower to collapse.

RIGHT: The presbytery vault dates from the early 16th century and is made of wood in imitation of the stone nave vault. The intersections of the main vault ribs are decorated with elaborately carved and coloured bosses depicting royal and episcopal heraldry and symbols of Christ's Passion.

Taken together, they called the observance of those seven occasions or 'hours' of prayer 'the Opus Dei' – the work of God. We might more easily understood that from the much used refrain, "As it was in the beginning is now and ever shall be…". The monks would remember how God was present in the past in his Christ; they would recall that He was also so present now, and seek to present to Him the world as it was in that particular moment, asking also that this present should grow into the future as He intended it. This prayer for the world is still the first task of the cathedral in the morning, at Evensong and during the day.

Entering the quire, the monks first, and then at intervals, turned towards the high altar, the crucifix and the Great Screen; alternately turning to face each other to sing the psalms and special texts for the day, each side answering the other. The rich foliage with animals and figures carved into their stalls is thought to have been created by William Lyngwode from Norfolk in about 1308. Each seat, when raised, is seen to have a ledge beneath it wonderfully carved – a misericord, used rather like a shooting stick as a more convenient perch when sitting and standing during the office. The quire is now closed at the west end by Sir George Gilbert Scott's screen (1875) in

RIGHT: The choirstall seats lift up to reveal misericords, small seats that allowed the monks to perch, half-standing and half-sitting, during the long hours of worship. Each has a different decorative subject and the Winchester misericords are, with few exceptions, completely non-religious and are a celebration of nature in all its forms.

RIGHT: William of Waynflete, Bishop of Winchester (1447–86), is buried in his chantry chapel in the retroquire, behind the Great Screen of which he was largely the patron. The chantry chapel would, with that of Waynflete's predecessor as Bishop, Cardinal Henry Beaufort, have flanked the 15th-century shrine of St Swithun.

BELOW: The screen that encloses the west end of the quire is the latest in a series of screens that have fulfilled that function. It was designed by Sir George Gilbert Scott to complement the 14th-century choirstalls and installed in 1874–5 in memory of two great churchmen of the 19th century, Dean Garnier of Winchester and Bishop Samuel Wilberforce.

RIGHT: The Great Screen was constructed during the episcopate of William Waynflete, probably between 1475 and 1490 and was originally populated with highly realistic figures of the cathedral's benefactors, Old Testament prophets and Saints and the crucified Christ. These were removed and mostly destroyed by Henry VIII's agents in the 1530s. Some fragments survive in the cathedral's Triforium Gallery and show what a wealth of art has been lost from our churches by religious reform. The sculpture we see on the screen today dates from the late 19th century.

OPPOSITE: The nucleus of the cathedral library is the book collection of George Morley, Bishop of Winchester (1662–84) and bequeathed to the Dean and Chapter for the use of the clergy of the Diocese of Winchester. Morley also left money in his will for the purchase of two globes, one terrestrial and one celestial. The contents of the room remain substantially the same as they appeared when installed after the bishop's death in 1684.

place of the Garbett Screen (1820), which replaced an earlier screen by Inigo Jones (1640), the central section of which is in the Museum of Archaeology and Anthropology in Cambridge.

At the east end, the quire is enclosed by the late 15th-century screen, niches of intricate carving supporting figures of saints, kings and bishops. The original figures were torn down and smashed by the reformers. Enough fragments remain and have been preserved in the Triforium Gallery to show that this must have been one of the great treasures of figurative carving. The damaged figure of the Virgin and Child, much sought after for major international exhibitions, is itself an indication of the genius of those unknown artists. The present figures were installed in the 19th century, which is how Queen Victoria came to join the distinguished assembly.

But in whichever age people came here to worship, the first focus was the Word of God's Love, spoken to all and represented with such devotion in the *Winchester Bible*, which can be seen in the Library. Now made up of four volumes (it was originally two), it was commissioned by Henry of Blois and was worked upon for at least 20 years by scribes and illustrators, using calf-skin, gold and pigments made from precious ingredients such as lapis lazuli.

RIGHT: The *Winchester Bible*, the centrepiece of the cathedral library, dates from the late 12th century and is one of the greatest surviving bibles from the early medieval period in the world. It was written on calf-skin vellum by one monk and illustrated over a period of 20 years by a team of international artists.

ABOVE: The initial from the opening of the *Old Testament* book, *The Song of Songs* in the *Winchester Bible*. The scene shows King Solomon and the Queen of Sheba sitting on a throne with their royal regalia. It was designed and painted by 'the Master of the Leaping Figures' in about 1165.

OPPOSITE: The nucleus of the cathedral library is the book collection of George Morley, Bishop of Winchester (1662–84) and bequeathed to the Dean and Chapter for the use of the clergy of the Diocese of Winchester. Morley also left money in his will for the purchase of two globes, one terrestrial and one celestial. The contents of the room remain substantially the same as they appeared when installed after the bishop's death in 1684.

place of the Garbett Screen (1820), which replaced an earlier screen by Inigo Jones (1640), the central section of which is in the Museum of Archaeology and Anthropology in Cambridge.

At the east end, the quire is enclosed by the late 15th-century screen, niches of intricate carving supporting figures of saints, kings and bishops. The original figures were torn down and smashed by the reformers. Enough fragments remain and have been preserved in the Triforium Gallery to show that this must have been one of the great treasures of figurative carving. The damaged figure of the Virgin and Child, much sought after for major international exhibitions, is itself an indication of the genius of those unknown artists. The present figures were installed in the 19th century, which is how Queen Victoria came to join the distinguished assembly.

But in whichever age people came here to worship, the first focus was the Word of God's Love, spoken to all and represented with such devotion in the *Winchester Bible*, which can be seen in the Library. Now made up of four volumes (it was originally two), it was commissioned by Henry of Blois and was worked upon for at least 20 years by scribes and illustrators, using calf-skin, gold and pigments made from precious ingredients such as lapis lazuli.

RIGHT: The *Winchester Bible*, the centrepiece of the cathedral library, dates from the late 12th century and is one of the greatest surviving bibles from the early medieval period in the world. It was written on calf-skin vellum by one monk and illustrated over a period of 20 years by a team of international artists.

ABOVE: The initial from the opening of the *Old Testament* book, *The Song of Songs* in the *Winchester Bible*. The scene shows King Solomon and the Queen of Sheba sitting on a throne with their royal regalia. It was designed and painted by 'the Master of the Leaping Figures' in about 1165.

Pilgrims – Past and Present

ABOVE: Flying buttresses were added to the south elevation of the nave at the end of the underpinning project of 1905–12 at the suggestion of the architect Sir Thomas Jackson.

OPPOSITE: The modern memorial to St Swithun stands on the site of his shrine, destroyed by Henry VIII's commissioners in 1538. It was designed by Brian Thomas and Wilfrid Carpenter Turner and installed in 1962, the 1100th anniversary of the saint's death.

RIGHT: The iconostasis, or series of icons, in the Orthodox tradition by Sergei Fyodorov was installed into the 14th-century screen in the retroquire between 1992 and 1996. The subjects comprise Christ, the Blessed Virgin Mary, St John the Baptist, the Saints Peter and Paul, the Archangels Gabriel and Michael and the Saints Birinus and Swithun.

LATE APRIL, ACCORDING TO CHAUCER, when travel became less fraught, was the season when an astonishing number of people began to set out on pilgrimage – a million a year it has been estimated, to Compostela alone. Seriously or, like Chaucer's pilgrims in part, on a jolly, they came to shrines such as that of St Swithun at Winchester. Looking after them in Pilgrims' Hall and the priory guest house was not only an act of charity but also a way of keeping law and order among a varied crowd of itinerant travellers, while the priory guest house, in the absence of modern hotels, provided for distinguished visitors and their entourage.

Why did pilgrims come here? Why do they come here still? Essentially a place of pilgrimage is a threshold place, where holiness is remembered, is still present and is to be touched by those who bring to it their own needs. Those who have suffered scant justice, hard rule and lived a hard life were here in touch with another kingdom and a welcome, when they entered the Holy Hole beneath the relics of St Swithun, or reached through the lunettes of the surround enclosing the tomb shrine created by the will of Cardinal Beaufort in 1476, where the iron memorial now stands. Here they left their prayers as a modern pilgrim may leave a lighted candle that remains burning long after they have gone on their way.

Here, too, the monks gathered in front of the shrine of their saint before a liturgical procession on great festivals, especially St Swithun's Day – still celebrated on July 15th each year.

Growing interest in Becket's shrine following his murder in 1170 drew away many of the pilgrim throng to Canterbury, so much so that Winchester had poor plunder for Thomas Cromwell's Commissioners in 1538. But the empty niches that once held figures of the great and good who were remembered here now house icons painted by the Russian icon painter Sergei Fyodorov, which were dedicated in January 1997 as the retroquire again became a consecrated place of prayer.

The Cathedral Today

ABOVE: The Girl Choristers rehearse in the practice room in The Pilgrims' School.

OPPOSITE: During their periods of residence the choir sings Evensong. At other times it is 'said' or sung by visiting choirs.

A FINE TEAM OF STAFF AND VOLUNTEERS makes a valued contribution to the cathedral as it seeks to serve church and diocese, city and county and the many who come here from further afield.

This is most obvious in the choral services on week days and Sundays with a choir of boys, chosen after voice trials, who receive an outstanding education at our own Choir School in the Close, Pilgrims' School, funded largely by the Chapter. Our girls' choir, drawn from young at our local schools, sing one service on a Sunday. All are trained by our Director of Music and Assistant with the help of an organ scholar. Both choirs are supported by a team of dedicated lay clerks. All are engaged in our prayer for the world and the service of the wide constituency of those we seek to serve.

But that is also true of those who greet you and seat you or who serve in the shop and the refectory, those high on the scaffolding or busy about the cathedral and Close, caring for it and putting it to rights, and the accounts department and other staff who keep it all solvent and running: people who value and build on the good work that has gone before and quietly sort out what was not perhaps so well done. You will find this too in the contemporary works of art in the cathedral, each of which also has a particular place in one or other of the festivals or occasions in our cycle of prayer. The cathedral is still a threshold place for those who come here, God's guests, ever seeking to serve them more faithfully and devotedly. For this is still, and shall be, a living cathedral. We hope you found a place here.

RIGHT: Mothers and their children, visitors and local people enjoy the sunshine on the terrace in the Visitors' Centre.

OVERLEAF CLOCKWISE FROM TOP LEFT: Members of the Verger's team prepare vestments for a service; bellringers in the ringing chamber; arranging flowers; children learn what it would have been like to have been a medieval Benedictine monk; members of the team of stonemasons use traditional methods of carving in their workshop; volunteers from parishes all over the Diocese of Winchester take turns to serve in the cathedral café.